THIS BOOK BELONGS TO:

_____

_____

EVERYDAY ACTIVIST

A Guided Journal for Engaging Your Community, Finding Your Voice, and Changing the World

TEXT BY
JESSICA JOLLIE

ILLUSTRATIONS BY
CAMILA ROSA

RP **STUDIO**

PHILADELPHIA

RP Studio™
Hachette Book Group
1290 Avenue of the Americas, New York, NY 10104
www.runningpress.com
@Running_Press

Printed in China

First Edition: March 2020

Published by RP Studio, an imprint of Perseus Books, LLC, a subsidiary of Hachette Book Group, Inc. The RP Studio name and logo is a trademark of the Hachette Book Group.

The publisher is not responsible for websites (or their content) that are not owned by the publisher.

Text by Jessica Jollie
Design by Rachel Peckman

ISBN: 978-0-7624-6863-8

LEO

10 9 8 7 6 5 4 3 2 1

CONTENTS

ENVIRONMENTAL

SOCIAL JUSTICE

POLITICAL

ISSUE-SPECIFIC ACTIVISM

INTRODUCTION

Welcome! You're almost ready to dive into the world of everyday activism—the steps, sometimes small and sometimes big, that we can all take to make our world a better, more just place.

But before we get started, I wanted to touch on the idea of willful ignorance; how those that choose to ignore or dismiss injustice can afford to do so as an exercise of privilege. This statement didn't feel original, so I Googled it just to make sure. It turns out, many authors (real authors, who do this sort of thing for a living) have written about willful ignorance as it applies to many of the topics you'll encounter in this journal, like racism and climate change, to name just a couple.

The fact that you've picked up this journal, and, hopefully, taken it home, means that you've already taken a step away from willful ignorance. Congratulations! You're on your way to doing your part.

This journal is all about small steps in activism, the kind that can and should be taken every day. Getting started can be daunting: With all that's going on in the world, it is easy to stare down the barrel of your newsfeed and feel overwhelmed, powerless, and out of control. It's easy to think that you are too small to make any sort of real impact—after all, you're just one person.

But you *can* make a real impact, and *Everyday Activist* is here to help. This journal is about you, that one person, taking action to create a practice of activism. It's about recognizing your strengths, skills, perseverance, and, yes, position of privilege, as you work to help others. The prompts and exercises in this book are with you every week—they're meant to help you think about what steps you can incorporate into your life sustainably, to live in a way that aligns with your values. Like any project—whether that's a fitness goal, an intricate meal, an art piece, a hike—you take small steps over a period of time, which ultimately get you there.

You'll find one prompt for each week of the year, covering a whole range of issues where you can make a difference. We'll look at ways to get active with the environment, social justice, and politics, as well as some more specific issues and situations where your help can make a big impact. Devote a little time each day to the week's activity, and record your progress, trimuphs, and challenges in the pages that follow. Each prompt is rated for difficulty with one, two, or three bullhorns. One bullhorn is going to be your easiest entry point—something that you can do from your bed with your pj's on. Two bullhorns are a little more involved, and require some effort and/or equipment to complete. And three bullhorns are the most involved—they might take some pre-planning, time, and equipment—but they're worth it!

There are only 52 weeks in a year, so you can bet that this journal isn't comprehensive in covering every single issue that plagues us. And the prompts were written by a person (me!), so you can bet that there is at least some amount of bias present. (I am a White and American Indian woman, millennial, citizen of the United States—just to put that on the table.) My goal in writing these prompts is to be inclusive and not policing; to have you push your boundaries in a sustainable way; and, hopefully, to introduce you to what will be a lifelong journey of learning, activism, and education.

Before we sally forth in this endeavor, know that you have full license to tailor this journey to you: because if you enjoy it, chances are, you'll keep doing it, which is the goal. Jump around from week to week. Use the lines as suggested, or as you see fit. Dig in, try something new, check-in with yourself. Research more.

Let's go.

SINGLE-USE PLASTICS

There's no denying it—plastic can be useful, and it's a ubiquitous part of every day: it's there when you grab a fork with your take out, when you're bagging your groceries, or when you buy a bottle of water at the gym. The environmental burden of plastic isn't as in-your-face, but it's very real. Thanks to serious consumption, there are five massive plastic "islands" floating around in the Pacific Ocean . . . and one is the size of Texas.

Take some time this week to write down every piece of single-use plastic that you throw away, down to each straw. Challenge yourself to replace some (or all!) of these items with reusable alternatives. At the end of the week, revisit your list and make notes on which changes you'll be able to incorporate into your life in a permanent way moving forward.

Need help getting started? Consider:

Reusable bags: Take time this week to put one in every purse, backpack, and messenger bag so you actually use them! Make a habit of bringing a bag with you (even when you likely won't need it).

Reusable cups, utensils, and water bottles: If you've looked back on your journal and notice that you are using a lot of these single-use items, it is definitely worth investing in a set.

Single-Use Plastics I Used

Changes I Can Make

COMPOSTING

DIFFICULTY:

Chances are that you and your household can cut down at least *some* of your total waste production by composting. It can be intimidating to get started—but ultimately (even if you live in a city!) composting really just means separating the organic material that you throw away from your normal trash, and creating certain conditions that cause that matter to decompose in a way that's beneficial for the environment.

This week, think about what composting could look like in your life. If you live in a more rural or suburban environment, designate an area of your yard to create a compost pile. If you live in a city, you might be able to find composting programs or services in your area with a quick internet search. Even if all the outdoor space you have is a window box, you can still compost yourself!

Use this space to brainstorm what you need to build composting into your routine. If you're composting in your own home, do you need to get a special bin? If you are participating in a composting service, what day do you need to drop off your materials? Are there restrictions on what can be composted in your area? If so, list them out so you don't forget! Think about these logistical pieces, then incorporate this practice into your everyday.

DISPOSABLE OUT, REUSABLE IN

DIFFICULTY: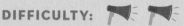

You've probably heard people talk about "throw-away culture." And this week, you'll do some work to think critically about what you and your household throw away, and what steps you can take to minimize this in the future.

Here are some examples of common disposable household items that can be replaced with reusable alternatives:

- **Cotton pads**
- **Make-up wipes**
- **Paper towels**
- **Disposable floor sweepers and mops**
- **Plastic produce bags**

Use the space on the next page to write down what you throw away, and challenge yourself to replace those items with more sustainable (recyclable, compostable) or reusable alternatives.

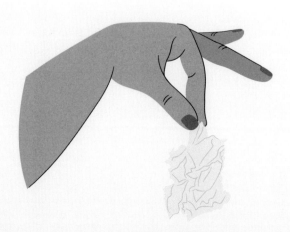

GET THERE GREENER

DIFFICULTY:

Getting from A to B is necessary, and oftentimes the way we go about it creates air pollution. You're not going to stop going places, so focus this week on making a concerted effort to do what you can to cut back on the pollution you create in your commute and day-to-day travels.

Getting to your destination in a more environmentally friendly way will look different for everyone: city folk should try and use public transportation or walk instead of taking a car service. If you live in the suburbs, challenge yourself to carpool. If you live in a rural area, plan to cut out one trip into town this week.

No matter where you live, this can be a tough one. Write down your thoughts on the following pages: Where were you able to reduce your travel-related environmental impact? How did your week of sustainable travel go? What surprised you? How are you going to incorporate this into your life moving forward?

BUY CARBON OFFSETS

DIFFICULTY:

Many of the things that you buy—from flights, to jeans, to postage—are sold by companies that offer carbon offsets. Though this isn't a comprehensive solution to climate change or even to reducing your emissions overall, it can be a good, low lift way to help you on the path to going carbon neutral.

Check out the National Resources Defense Council (www.nrdc.org) for a comprehensive guide on choosing the right carbon offsets, and keep track of the most important factors to consider. In the meantime, check the option to "make this purchase green" this week when you're buying online. Make a note of the websites that you found that offer offsets, to use as a reference later.

WEBSITES

_____

_____

_____

_____

_____

_____

Notes

FARMERS AND GARDENS WEEK

DIFFICULTY: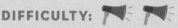

Buying locally grown and produced food has many great benefits for your community: it helps support local businesses, cuts down on pollution caused by transportation, is more sustainable, and, in general, is just tastier. Though this option is sometimes less convenient than your grocery store, try buying your groceries this week from a farmers' market. If this is too much of a stretch for you, try just buying your produce locally this week. Use the boxes on the next page to make a list of what is grown in your area during the different seasons, and how you can incorporate these foods into your meal planning.

Need help finding local growers in your area? Check out www.localharvest.org to find farms in your zip code. If there aren't growers in your area, do some research around what produce or foods you can grow yourself where you live! Whether you have space for a row of kale or just a window box of herbs, this is simply about doing what you can to eat food grown locally.

WINTER

SPRING

SUMMER

FALL

Farms to Know

Produce to Grow and Meals to Make

BAD HABIT WEEK

We all have one: either you don't turn off all the lights when you leave the house, or throw away something that you know could probably be recycled: Challenge yourself this week to kick that *one* habit. Write down reminders for yourself and tape them to your mirror and front door, or program them into your phone—whatever you have to do to start making a practice of kicking your bad habit.

Use the space below to brainstorm your bad environmental habits, and circle the one you'll focus on this week. What are three methods to hold yourself accountable for kicking this?

HABITS

Methods

Reflections

VEGGIE WEEK

DIFFICULTY: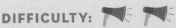

Though it is difficult to parse out which particular farming practices lead to which environmental effects, it is pretty clear that the meat industry uses more water and land, and also produces more waste, than vegetable farming. Meat production, especially large-scale farming, is also a big contributor to greenhouse gas emissions.

This week, challenge yourself by cooking and eating completely vegetarian. (Too easy? Try going vegan! The dairy industry produces plenty of carbon too.)

Use the space that follows to do some meal planning. For each day, write down what you'll be having for your meals, and your grocery list. At the end of the week make sure to reflect on how the challenge felt: Were any particular meals difficult? Was it hard to eat meat-free at restaurants? How can you adapt your diet moving forward to be just a little more plant-based?

MONDAY

TUESDAY

WEDNESDAY

THURSDAY

FRIDAY

SATURDAY/SUNDAY

Reflections

POSITIVE VIBES IN THE NATURAL WORLD

DIFFICULTY:

As you go about each day this week, think about one thing in the natural world that you encountered that was beautiful, or gave you joy. Often we think of the places that we live, particularly if those places are more urban, as completely separate from "nature." Ultimately, noticing, respecting, and thanking the natural world we encounter every day will help us be more aware of our individual impact on it. When you see litter, pick it up. Walk on sidewalks instead of the grass. Even small changes add up.

Use this space to write down one thing about the natural world that gave you joy each day. For an extra challenge, list one thing each day that you can do to foster a more positive impact on your environment.

MONDAY

TUESDAY

WEDNESDAY

THURSDAY

FRIDAY

SATURDAY/SUNDAY

#SCIENCE WEEK

If you happen to be one of the warriors doing research and work to help understand climate change and protect our environment and communities, thank you!

If not, set up a recurring donation to a group doing important work to protect the environment. Take a moment to look at each of the organizations suggested below, or do your own research and write notes to keep track of the causes you're interested in supporting.

- **350.org**
- **Environment America**
- **Union of Concerned Scientists**
- **Citizens Climate Lobby**
- **Conservation International**
- **Environmental Defense Fund**
- **Sierra Club**
- **The Nature Conservancy**
- **League of Conservation Voters**
- **World Wildlife Fund**

To deepen your research and commitment to the environment, make a pledge to stay informed! Here are some organizations to subscribe to and learn more about (these are just the tip of the Iceberg!)

- **Climate Impact Lab**
- **Climate Solutions: Stanford EARTH**
- **International Institute for Environment and Development**

Notes

WATER WEEK

Water is precious, and even though your tap may overfloweth, this resource is not unlimited. According to the United States Environmental Protection Agency, 80 percent of state water managers in the U.S. expect water shortages in the coming years (if it hasn't started happening already where you live).

This week, focus on ways you can reduce your water usage, and write down your actions on the following pages. Here are some tips and suggestions:

- **Wash clothes on low-energy setting, and hand-wash where you can. Not only does this reduce water usage, but it also helps prevent tiny fabric particles from your clothes from being released into the ocean.**

- **If you wash dishes one-by-one, switch to what we'll call the "basin" method: Fill up your sink with soapy water and wash dishes in batches—it uses less water!**

DIFFICULTY:

For an added (and informative!) challenge, actually time your showers, and see if you can cut down your showers by 1–5 minutes each day. Keep track of your progress on the next page!

Shower Times

MONDAY

TUESDAY

WEDNESDAY

THURSDAY

FRIDAY

SATURDAY/SUNDAY

My Water Conservation Steps

SAVE!

RECYCLING WEEK

DIFFICULTY:

Recycling is something that's been around for a while—
chances are you've thrown something plastic into a designated
bin every once in a while, or perhaps make a point to
recycle regularly.

Whatever the case may be, take some time this week
to research what is actually recyclable in your area—you
might be surprised! Write down the restrictions below so
you can refer back and be on top of your day-to-day
recycling at home.

MY LOCAL RECYCLING RULES

DIFFICULTY:

Make a point to recycle as much as you can this week,
including items that take a little bit of extra effort, like
takeout food containers. Rinse out all containers that can be
recycled. Any items that might otherwise be recyclable are
not if they still have food material in them (e.g. greasy pizza
boxes). Record what you recycled on the following pages.

MONDAY

TUESDAY

WEDNESDAY

THURSDAY

FRIDAY

SATURDAY/SUNDAY

Reflections

PLANT SOMETHING

DIFFICULTY: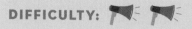

The natural world is beautiful—contribute to that beauty this week! Plant something, either in your own home, your yard, or at your local park or playground with an organization that supports green spaces.

DIFFICULTY:

For a lighter lift, you could contribute to an organization that plants trees in your area, or your community garden. A quick look on your preferred search engine will show a variety of organizations that do just this!

Write (or draw!) what you or your dollars planted below:

_____

_____

_____

_____

_____

_____

_____

SUSTAINABILITY, BUT MAKE IT FASHION

DIFFICULTY: 📣 📣 📣

Like single-use plastics, or the meat and dairy industries, almost everyone interacts with the fashion industry in some way. The fashion world itself produces a lot of carbon and waste—this week, focus in on your interactions with this industry, and see if you can take steps to limit waste. Here are someome ideas to get you started:

- **Buy vintage or pre-owned clothing instead of fast fashion— you'll be cutting down on wasted materials and the pollution associated with clothing production.**

- **Up-cycle items you already own (e.g. turn your ripped, too short jeans into cut-offs, or use some old, worn-out clothes as dusting cloths).**

- **Buy from sustainable clothing stores. This is a trend that's picking up more and more steam—with good reason. Brands like Everlane, Reformation, J. Crew, and H&M (and more!) have launched sustainable, and well-priced, clothing options for consumers looking to minimize their impact on the environment.**

In the space below, think about what clothing items you're likely to buy in the coming week, month, or season. Think about ways you could achieve that look with items you already own, or make a plan to buy a more sustainable alternative. If there are clothes that no longer suit your needs or style, brainstorm some ways to make sure they get a second life, either through donation or up-cycling.

THE "BUBBLE" WEEK

Chances are you have something of a routine in your life. You live in a particular neighborhood, commute on a particular route, and go to a certain grocery store. We all live in a microcosm of people, but we rarely take the time to think critically or actually document the types of people we surround ourselves with, consciously and unconsciously. As you go about your life this week, make note of the people around you, and whether you're seeing diversity in the following categories:

• **Gender identity**

• **Race or ethnic group**

• **Age**

NOTES

NOTES

Challenge yourself to find a new place where you are around different kinds of people. Check in with yourself: How did you feel in that space? How did you conduct yourself in that space that felt different? Is there anything that you will take with you/do differently moving forward? Are there ways you can learn from the new groups you interacted with? How can you do so with respect? Use the space on the next pages to work through your thoughts.

CONTENT WEEK

What kinds of content do you consume? Think about the books that you read and the movies and TV you watch. What about your YouTube, Instagram, and FaceBook feeds? What about the music you listen to? Jot down your lists on the next page.

Now take a moment to think about the things you wrote down. Are you following people who don't look like you, or people who have had different life experiences than you have? Do you consume content from people who challenge your worldview in a productive way? Does the content you consume encourage a more expansive, inclusive, or justice-oriented way of thinking?

Think about these questions as you look at your newsfeed this week, and challenge yourself to make adjustments accordingly. One tip to help expand the content you consume: follow authors and/or journalists, and look at who they follow in turn. You can also use this method to seek out activists featured in more mainstream publications.

Content I Consume

Reflections

SPEAK UP

DIFFICULTY: 📣

This week, challenge yourself, even just once, to have *that* conversation—about race, politics, feminism, or some other "taboo" but important topic. See some ideas below:

- **Engage in a conversation on a difficult topic with a friend whom you trust, but maybe haven't ever "gone there" with.**

- **When someone you love (or don't!) says something that is racist/sexist/transphobic/homophobic, call them out. Make a practice of this.**

- **Instead of posting your views about a topic on social media, make a point to bring it up in person to the people you interact with that day.**

Make a note below each time you spoke up this week. How did you feel after each interaction? Did it get easier or harder with practice?

💬 _____

💬 _____

💬 _____

💬 _____

💬 _____

💬 _____

💬 _____

💬 _____

Reflections

HELP INDIVIDUALS AND FAMILIES WITH YOUR DOLLARS

Spend some time this week on GoFundMe, Facebook, local newsletters, or wherever your neighborhood congregates online, to find actual individuals and families in your area that need help. Give what you can, even if it's one dollar.

If you're having trouble picking who to give to, think: "What privileges do I have, and what can I offer to people who don't have that privilege?"

If you're having trouble finding someone to give to, you can search hashtags like #Reparations, to find links to give. Write down where your money, or other resources, went below.

PUT YOUR MONEY WHERE YOUR MOUTH IS

DIFFICULTY:

You speak with your voice, your actions, and also your resources: this week, look at where you spend money. Using the space below, reflect on your credit card or bank statement from the last month. List your top ten transactions, by frequency *and* highest dollar amount spent, and think about these questions:

- Am I supporting businesses that prioritize diversity and are diversely-owned?

- Am I supporting businesses that give back to my community, have ethical manufacturing, and support or promote causes that I also support?

Commit to spending some time researching the top three places where you spend your money (or more, if you're looking for an extra challenge) and record what you find. Even if you make changes to your spending patterns with just one place, you'll be making an impact!

Tip: When looking for better places to spend your money, look for 501(b) corporations, or "B Corps," as they are certified and held to higher standards in terms of social and environmental performance, as well as financial transparency.

1.

2.

3.

4.

5.

6.

7.

8.

9.

10.

Research

FACILITATE REGULAR CONVERSATION

DIFFICULTY: 📣 📣 📣

Safe spaces are integral to building community, sharing new ideas, and forging new friendships. This week, focus on facilitating a space to hold regular conversations with the people around you. This space can be anything you want—a feminist book club, coffee-tasting group, Weekly Wine Wednesdays. All that matters is that it is a place where you, friends, and soon-to-be friends can meet and talk openly and productively. Use the space on the pages that follow to dream up the gathering you'd like to create. Jot down a few ideas and start organizing to make it happen! Pick a date, time, and location, and write down three people you can invite. Ask each of those people to bring one friend.

If you already facilitate regular conversation, that's awesome! Challenge yourself to bring a few new people into the fold this week, or take your group out to volunteer in your larger community.

PEOPLE TO BRING

THINGS TO DISCUSS

STEP UP, STEP BACK

DIFFICULTY: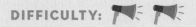

Speaking up for yourself, and encouraging those whose voices are heard less often to speak up in turn, is critical when making change anywhere. This week, as you find yourself in a group setting, focus in on the concept of "Step Up, Step Back." If you notice that you are the underrepresented person in the room, step up and add your voice to the conversation. If you find that you aren't, step back and support the voice of someone who is underrepresented. What can you do to lift up the voice of someone who doesn't share your same privileges?

Write about the groups you belong to below, and circle whether you should focus on stepping up, or stepping back.

STEP UP | STEP BACK

STEP UP | STEP BACK

STEP UP | STEP BACK

STEP UP | STEP BACK

STEP UP,
STEP BACK!

VOLUNTEER

DIFFICULTY: 📣 📣 📣

This journal asks you to meditate (a lot) about which points of privilege you occupy, and how to leverage those points of privilege to help lift up those people who don't share them. This week, apply this concept to volunteering. What unique skill can you bring to your community?

Here are some ideas and resources:

Mentoring: Whether you go through a program like Big Brother or Big Sister, or work with a local school, this directly uses your abilities to foster those skills in someone else!

Volunteer with your profession: Whether you utilize your accounting skills at organizations that need help filing their taxes, or you serve as a lawyer for a non-profit, this can be a great way to find your niche in giving back.

Head to www.volunteermatch.org, your nearest university or school, or a local charity, to research opportunities.

Use the pages that follow to plot out where you'll volunteer this week. When will you be going back?

_____

_____

_____

_____

MODEL POSITIVE BEHAVIOR FOR THE NEXT GENERATION

DIFFICULTY:

Even if you don't have kids, modeling positive, inclusive behaviors for the young people you encounter has its benefits. Whether it's a random child you pass by in the street, or a teenager you interact with while going about your daily errands, the kind of behaviors you engage in makes an impact. Interact with people with respect, follow traffic laws and crosswalks, and say please and thank you. Think about how you can encourage positive behaviors in young people through your own actions.

MY ACTIONS

DIFFICULTY: 📣 📣

If you have little ones in your life, consider sending them children's' books that feature characters and stories from diverse races and cultures. Take some time this week to talk to them about the hard topics: white privilege, racism, socio-economic injustice. Kids are really just tiny humans, who will one day grow into big humans. We shouldn't shy away from the tough stuff. List some topics below.

On the next page, write down a memory from your childhood when you learned about or encountered some of these important topics. Why has this memory stuck with you? How does it impact your life now? How can you use this memory to inform your interactions with young people?

_____

_____

_____

_____

_____

_____

_____

_____

BE A GOOD NEIGHBOR

DIFFICULTY:

In this transient world, it can sometimes feel like we don't live in tight-knit communities, even when we share walls with those around us. This week, make an effort to talk to your neighbors, or do something nice for them to show your support. If you can't interact with neighbors directly, engage otherwise in your community by joining a community Facebook group, or some other local newsletter—or, if one doesn't exist already, consider starting one yourself.

Below, write down three new things (they can be people, or facts) that you learned about your neighborhood this week.

1.

2.

3.

Reflections

LOCAL NEWS

DIFFICULTY:

Plug in to your local news, preferably your local newspapers, newsletters, and magazines. (Local TV news can be great, but many channels are owned by large conglomerates and can harbor biases. A good rule of thumb here is that seeking out more perspectives allows you to discern facts and shape your own opinion more easily.) Educate yourself on local issues, problems, and resources.

In the space below, write down some issues that are affecting your community, as seen through the lens of local news media. Were you already aware of them, or are you hearing about them for the first time? How does this information change the way you interact with your community going forward?

LOCAL ISSUES

BECOME A "COMMUNITY AMBASSADOR"

This week, focus on becoming an encyclopedia of the resources/go-to places in your community. See if you can find out the answers to all of the prompts below.

Where does someone in my community go to address . . .

FOOD INSECURITY

SHELTER

CLOTHING/BASIC GOODS

MEDICAL HELP

A GOOD CUP OF COFFEE

MENTAL HEALTH SERVICES

MENTORING RESOURCES

VOLUNTEERING OPPORTUNITIES

OTHER COMMUNITY RESOURCES

REMEMBER THE GREATS, SUPPORT OTHER ACTIVISTS

The truth is, every step that we take in our activism, big or small, was made possible by activists in the past (and today!) doing the same work, and opening doors wider for us. This week, think about the activists that you know or are on your radar, and support their work—leave a nice comment on a social media post, tell your friends and neighbors about the work of activists you admire, or make a monetary contribution to their work.

Think about the issues you care about most: Who has paved the way in how we think about these topics? Write their name(s) below. How are you inspired by them? Think about them each day this week, as you move forward in your life and activism.

REMEMBER the GREATS!

KNOW YOUR STATS

If someone were to ask you who represents you politically on the national level, odds are you probably know the answer—you know who to hold accountable. It's just as important to know who your elected representatives are on a local level, as the decisions that these leaders make have a daily impact on your life, and the lives of those around you. This week, dedicate time to research which districts you live in and who currently represents you in those districts. Challenge yourself to fill out all of the following that apply to you:

STATE AND GOVERNOR

SENATORS

HOUSE OF REPRESENTATIVES

STATE LEGISLATURE

COUNTY AND COUNTY LEGISLATORS

CITY/MUNICIPALITY COUNCIL

PRECINCT

SCHOOL DISTRICT

ELECTED JUDGES

For an extra challenge: research more about the representatives that hold these offices. Are they affiliated with a political party? How long have they held office? What have they voted for or against? Are there questions you'd like to see them answer, or issues you'd like to have them tackle? Record what you find on the pages that follow.

REGISTER TO VOTE

DIFFICULTY:

If you're not currently registered to vote, just do it. If you have moved recently (or not so recently!) and think you might not be registered to vote where you currently live, call your local Board of Elections and find out your status. Do the same if you've had any other major life changes, like a new name or party affiliation.

Make a note below of the steps and requirements to register in your area—it might be helpful to pass along this information to someone you know in the future!

HOST A VOTER REGISTRATION DRIVE

What are the communities that you belong to? (Think church, neighborhood, book club, or any of the constituencies you wrote down on p. 86!)

Talk to the powers that be in these groups about setting up a voter registration drive. Research the registration requirements in your area, either by looking online or meeting with your local Board of Elections officials to get a training on how to handle forms and fill them out.

Registering to vote/voting is the most important thing we can do to enact the change we want in the world around us. The right to vote is critical, and registering someone to vote is incredibly important, as it empowers them to participate in our democracy. There are also important logistical considerations for you to keep in mind when you decide to help register others to vote. Depending on the state where you live, it can be a felony to mishandle a voter registration form, so make sure you do the leg work to understand the proper protocol here before you dive in!

Write down the materials you need to have your voter registration drive, and how you'll get those materials. Consider writing down some language you'll use when trying to get people to register. Make a note of which day you're doing it, and recruit a friend to help you out!

Materials

Talking Points

Address, Date, Time and Logistics

VIGILANTE VOTER REGISTRATION WEEK

DIFFICULTY:

This week, it's time to tackle voter registration, vigilante style. Have a blank voter registration form with you in your bag, at all times. Keep them in the glove compartment of your car, or in a drawer at work, to be deployed to that colleague that just moved, the friend who "hasn't gotten around to it yet," or the person you meet in line at the post office.

Be your friendly, neighborhood voting evangelist: challenge yourself to register even one new person this week, and keep a tally.

Important Note: Similar to "Host a Voter Registration Drive" week on p. 92, this challenge requires research and knowing your stuff. Make sure to sit down with your local Board of Elections to know the ins and outs of voter registration before you do this, plan your strategy and record your research on the next page.

KNOW YOUR DATES!

DIFFICULTY: 📣

This week, take some time to make note of voter registration deadlines, election days, and crucial meetings in your area. Put them in your calendar, and set a reminder. Write them down for a quick reference guide, post about them on social media, and text your friends when they come up.

PUT YOUR MONEY WHERE YOUR MOUTH IS: ELECTION DAY EDITION

DIFFICULTY:

Elections are a time when using your dollars in service of your activism can have a big impact!

In a Primary Election: Pick an office and donate to the candidate(s) who resonates with you most, and aligns with your values. Spend some time this week reading a diverse array of coverage on the candidates, as this is a good way to hear the voices and positions of different candidates.

It is also a good idea to take time to read up on all the candidates, including the less well-known ones—even if it's just a quick browse on their campaign websites or Twitter feeds. Sometimes, for a variety of reasons, some candidates don't receive as much coverage as others—but that doesn't mean you shouldn't donate your energy or resources to them Record what you learn below.

_____

_____

_____

_____

_____

In a General Election: Research your candidates in the same way, but think a little more globally. Pay attention to political parties and endorsements from organizations and individuals you trust! Write your findings below, and keep track of the dollar amounts of any donations for your records.

DONATE YOUR TIME

DIFFICULTY:

This week, pick a campaign or candidate that resonates with you, and donate your time. Most campaigns need as many people as possible to reach out to voters, both door-to-door and over the phone. This is incredibly important work, and like most important things, can be a little scary the first time you do it. If you're hesitant about getting started, challenge yourself to at least give it a try for one hour, either in person or by phone. If you still don't feel comfortable, then you can get involved in a variety of other ways! Here are some ideas for contributing your time and energy:

- **Text for a campaign. This is easy as pie, and a very effective way to get in touch with voters.**

- **Bring food to a local field office for other volunteers and campaign workers.**

- **Clean a local field office (this task is often last on the priority list, and when campaign staffers are done with their day at 9:00PM, the last thing they want to do is vacuum).**

- **Offer to help sign in and train other volunteers on a weekend morning.**

- **Have a spare room? Host a campaign staffer! These staffers are often young, moving around, and in need of places to stay when they are on assignment for a campaign in your area.**

DATE

TIME

ACTION

CAMPAIGN

DATE

TIME

ACTION

CAMPAIGN

Reflections

BRING A FRIEND

This week, when you are out volunteering and making a difference with the campaign of your choice (registering voters, bringing a casserole to a field office, going for a canvassing shift for your favorite city council candidate), bring a friend who is interested but has never gotten involved before. Not only will this make volunteering 1000% more fun, it doubles your impact and grows the movement.

Below, write down the names of three friends who might be interested in helping your campaign or candidate. Next to their names, write the day, time, and method you'll use to get in contact with them. Put a check mark next to their names when you've reached out.

NAME

DATE

TIME

METHOD

NAME

DATE

TIME

METHOD

NAME

DATE

TIME

METHOD

Reflections

C4 WEEK

If you've already made room in your budget for a donation to an organization whose work you love, chances are that Organization has c3 status, making that donation tax deductible (which is awesome). This week, consider making a one-time donation to an organization's c4 arm (lots of organizations that we know and love, like Planned Parenthood, have these). C4s are able to get a little more political, so while your dollar isn't going directly to a particular candidate or political party that you choose yourself, and the contribution isn't tax deductible, it does help the organization itself spend resources on candidates and/or parties that are doing work that aligns with theirs.

Do a brainstorm below and on the pages that follow. What are some organizations that you know, love, and already donate to? Do a little research on their website to see if they have a c4 arm that you can donate to, and make a plan to incorporate them into your giving.

_____

_____

_____

_____

_____

WRITE YOUR REP

 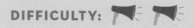

Remember all that work you did researching your representatives on p. 86? As a constituent, when you have feedback, positive or negative, it makes an impact to let your representative know what that feedback is. On your representative's "official" web page they will often have an email or a physical address where you can send written correspondence. You should also consider calling—representatives notice when their staff are tied up on the phones.

Write down your representative's address and phone number below for quick access, and brainstorm some topics you'd like to offer thoughts on. When are you planning to reach out this week? What has been on your mind as a constituent?

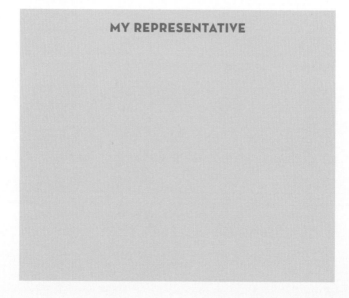

MY REPRESENTATIVE

MY CONCERNS

GET INVOLVED WITH YOUR LOCAL POLITICAL INFRASTRUCTURE

Often, even if you're politically active, you'll tend to concentrate your involvement during election season. But most political parties and groups have regular events, fundraisers, or socials that happen all year round. Challenge yourself to find what's out there this week, and attend! Even better—bring a friend!

Like most political activism, getting involved with your local political infrastructure can take many different forms. You can volunteer at your local county party headquarters, attend the regular meetings, or even run for a leadership role. Sustained involvement in political organizations is how you foster long term change. Use the space below to note where your party HQ is located,and take notes on your research (or notes from the meeting you attended!)

_____

_____

_____

_____

_____

Notes

THE CENSUS AND WHERE YOU LIVE

DIFFICULTY:

The census is important! It is only conducted once every ten years and impacts how the government works for an entire decade. Know when the census is coming and fill it out when it arrives. Even if the census isn't happening right this very moment, there is still important and interesting information about your community that you can find as a result of it.

Go to: www.census.gov and enter your zip code to learn about your community. Fill out your findings below. Is there anything that surprises you, or motivates you to get more involved?

POPULATION

NUMBER OF WOMEN

NUMBER OF VETERANS

MEAN TRAVEL TO WORK TIME IN MINUTES

A SURPRISING STATISTIC

WHAT MAKES YOUR COMMUNITY TICK

DIFFICULTY: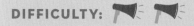

This week, discover the local groups that work within your community to help it function. Look up when your local community governing groups meet, and show up to a meeting. If you live in the city, this could be your neighborhood governance group; if you live in a more rural area, this could be your school board or chamber of commerce. Take notes below from the meeting. Even if you just go once, you'll learn more about the folks doing the work in your area, and might be inspired to be more involved moving forward.

GROUP

MEETING TYPE

DATE

LOCATION

PURPOSE

Notes

NATURAL DISASTERS

Climate change is real, and scientists know that one of the effects of it is natural disasters becoming more frequent and destructive. When something like this happens, or even when there isn't a specific climate event, here are some ways to get involved and help:

• **Donate to the Red Cross. When disasters strike, it is important to give to an organization that has the infrastructure to act fast.**

• **Donate to people who are affected directly. GoFundMe is a way to give to people, families, and local groups in the affected area.**

This week, check-in with yourself about what you are doing in your everyday life to reduce your impact on the environment. What lifestyle changes have you made that are going well? What could you improve on?

WHAT I'VE DONE

WHAT I COULD DO BETTER

Reflections

WHEN SOMETHING HAPPENS IN YOUR COMMUNITY

DIFFICULTY:

Important, sometimes life changing, events happen in our communities and neighborhoods every day, whether it's an issue that's playing out on the national stage, or one that only gets coverage in your neighborhood Facebook group. If it's a cause that resonates with you, you should lean in and do what you can to help. Research whether there are local fundraisers or Go Fund Me pages set up, or offer to volunteer to organize donations (whether monetary or of materials like food or clothing.) If someone you know—or even someone you don't know that well—is affected, reach out and offer a listening ear.

Using the space on the next page, write down what's going on in your community. What are your neighbors talking about? What's on their minds? How can you be of service to others?

GUN VIOLENCE

This is an issue that rears its head in many different ways across our country and world. Everytown and Moms Demand Action are great organizations to follow on the national level to stay informed when crucial legislation relating to this issue is on the floor in Congress.

It's important to also remain diligent locally—research in your local print news media about gun violence in your community. Reach out to your mayor's office, or other local officials, to find out what they're doing to help keep your community safe.

DIFFICULTY:

Make a note of the relevant legislation and organizations in your area. Are there ways you can become more involved, whether by calling your elected officials before votes or by joining an activist group? Reflect on how you want to raise awareness of this issue, and help those who are most affected, whether in your local community or elsewhere.

MARCH

DIFFICULTY: 📣 📣

Are you ready to march? In our current moment, there is a different protest or march every week—and often more than one! If you find yourself overwhelmed, remember that making a *practice* of showing up, for *different* causes, on a *regular basis*, can be the most impactful action of all. Is there a cause that you follow on Instagram but don't really participate in, or an activist hashtag that you're curious about? Research that group, and speak with a member about when their next march or rally is. Ask a member of the group how you can help, and brainstorm some ideas on the next page for getting more involved.

Are there any demonstrations, marches, or meetings you can show up to this week? Write them down and make a plan to show up. Make a packing list for the day, including sunscreen, rain gear, and any signage you want to bring!

THIS WEEK'S DEMONSTRATIONS

MY PACKING LIST

Notes

WEEK-LONG DEEP DIVE

DIFFICULTY:

This week, pick one issue and read all that you can find about it online or at your local library. The goal here is to give yourself space to learn the ins and outs of one issue that you might not have had time to dig into previously—who knows, you might even change your opinion. Write your notes below, including any ideas for getting active on a more regular basis with this cause!

MY ISSUE

_____

_____

_____

WHY I CARE

_____

_____

_____

_____

My Research

MASS INCARCERATION

DIFFICULTY:

This week, educate yourself about this important issue. The American Civil Liberties Union is a great place to start, as they have comprehensive and easily digestible information about mass incarceration in the United States. You can sign up for their text alerts to keep yourself in the know about when important legislation regarding this issue comes to the floor of Congress, and what you can do to help.

Other ways to act include signing petitions to show support for legislation, and, of course, donating. You can also research halfway houses and other resources for people returning to your community from prison. Do you have a skill or a resource to offer returning individuals? Can you donate money or needed items? Brainstorm some ideas below, and reflect on how you can be an ally in ending mass incarceration and aiding with reentry.

PUBLIC HEALTH CRISIS

DIFFICULTY:

This one is big. Public health touches each of us and the people we love in different ways: addiction, lack of insurance, underinsurance, the high cost of prescription drugs, elder care, rural healthcare, racism in the healthcare system—the list goes on.

This week, take some time to think and write about the ways that you interact with the healthcare system. If you are a healthcare worker, think critically about the way you interact with your patients. If you aren't, learn about the health insurance exchange where you live. How would you get coverage if you lost your job, or if you were self-employed? Reach out to your state representatives and/or governor's office, to learn about what they are doing to make improvements to your options for healthcare.

EDUCATION

This week, take the time to research local schools in your area. Contact them, see what, they need and learn what you (and your network) can do to help! Some ideas below:

• **Donating school supplies or money**

• **Providing mentorship**

• **Volunteering**

• **Participating in school fundraisers**

• **Running for School Board**

SCHOOLS LOCAL TO ME

DIFFICULTY:

Visit the websites of the National Education Association or the National Federation of Teachers to see what you can do in your area to support the goals of the two largest teachers' unions in the U.S.

Use the next page to plan your action, take notes, or write more generally about how the education system has impacted your life. You can write about a teacher, club, or even a fellow student! How can you use that experience to support schools in your area today?

WOMEN'S RIGHTS

DIFFICULTY: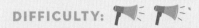

Advocating for women's equality is an ongoing mission—one that can be reflected in your everyday actions and your activism. Tackle both ends of the spectrum this week.

On a personal level, think about the amazing women in your life, and write down their names below. A rising tide lifts all boats, so challenge yourself to reach out proactively to lift one woman in your life up this week. Brainstorm how you can help, whether that's a cup of coffee and a listening ear, a job contact, or a small gift.

On a more macro level, think about your feminism: How do your actions reflect a feminist world view? Does your feminism include black, indigenous, and other people of color? Does it include trans women? Reflect on what being a feminist means to you, and how you can work to make your feminism more inclusive and intersectional.

AMAZING WOMEN IN MY LIFE

WHAT BEING A FEMINIST MEANS TO ME

INDIGENOUS RIGHTS

DIFFICULTY: 📢

Whose land are you on?

This week, before every hike (on a mountain or to the office) research the indigenous tribe(s) whose land it was before colonization. Write the names of those indigenous groups on the next page. What are those tribal members doing now and how can you support them and pay reparations? Are there indigenous-owned businesses that you can support? Can you donate to causes that lift up indigenous voices and issues (e.g. Native American Philanthropy)? Make a plan to actively support indigenous communities in your area, and educate yourself on any legislation that may be impacting their rights.

INDIGENOUS TRIBES

WHAT I CAN DO TO SUPPORT

My Plan

HEALTHCARE WORKERS AND FIRST RESPONDERS

DIFFICULTY:

First responders are the first people to help in an emergency. You might not think too much about their presence until you need them. This week, do your research—what are the local fire stations and hospitals in your area? Donate to them, sign up for their newsletters or publications, volunteer, or just send in the staff flowers or a treat. And record their locations here, to reference in case you ever need them.

Use the space on the following pages to think about those who have helped you in an emergency. Maybe they're a first responder, or just a friend. Remember them here, and send them some kindness this week.

MY FIRST RESPONDERS

FIRE STATION

HOSPITALS

OTHERS

SELF-CARE: TAKING RESPONSIBILITY FOR, AND LOVING, YOURSELF

Self-care is a form of activism. You are a steward of the world around you and the causes you care about, so you should make sure to take care of yourself to ensure that you can continue all your hard work. Take one (or more than one) night this week to do *exactly* what it is you want to do and use the space below to plan.

Some ideas to get you started:

- Cancel on the dinner plans and grab takeout (ideally with your own container and reusable flatware).

- Go to that play/exhibition/bar/restaurant you've been meaning to go to.

- Go for a run or to the gym . . . or skip that workout you've been dreading.

- Go to bed early this week. Get some much needed rest to think more clearly.

- Dedicate at least one hour each day to personal betterment, like:

  - BUDGETING
  - JOB SEARCH/RESEARCH
  - NETWORKING

This Week I Will

RESOURCES

A note for readers: By now, you're well on your way to making a practice of activism in your life. Below is a compilation of resources for you to use in your journey. Some of the organizations below have been mentioned in the pages of this journal, and some are included here for further consideration. This list is by no means comprehensive—which is a good thing! There's a lot to uncover! Use this as a starting point for further research and learning.

Environmental

LEARN MORE AND GET INVOLVED

- 350.org
- Climate Impact Lab: impactlab.org
- Climate Solutions: Stanford EARTH: earth.stanford.edu/research/climate-solutions
- Conservation International: conservation.org
- Environment America: environmentamerica.org
- Environmental Defense Fund: edf.org
- Green Latinos: greenlatinos.org
- International Institute for Environment and Development: iied.org
- National Ocean and Atmospheric Administration: oceanservice.noaa.gov
- Natural Resources Defence Council: nrdc.org
- Sierra Club: sierraclub.org
- The Nature Conservancy: nature.org
- Union of Concerned Scientists: ucsusa.org
- World Wildlife Fund: worldwildlife.org/

Social Justice

LEARN MORE AND GET INVOLVED

- American Civil Liberties Union: aclu.org
- Amnesty International: amnesty.org
- Black Lives Matter: blacklivesmatter.com/
- Essence Communications: essence.com/about/
- IllumiNatives: illuminatives.org
- NAACP: naacp.org/about-us/
- NARAL: prochoiceamerica.org
- National Association of Women Business Owners: nawbo. org
- Planned Parenthood: plannedparenthood.org
- Southern Poverty Law Center: splcenter.org
- Volunteer Match: volunteermatch.com

Political

LEARN MORE

- US Census: census.gov
- US Electoral Process: usa.gov/election

GET INVOLVED

- Citizens Climate Lobby: citizensclimatelobby.org
- Democratic Socialists of America: dsausa.org
- Indivisible: indivisible.org/
- League of Conservation Voters: lcv.org
- Move On: front.moveon.org/
- Town Hall Project: townhallproject.com/

Issue-Specific Activism

LEARN MORE AND GET INVOLVED

- American Civil Liberties Union: aclu.org
- American Red Cross: redcross.org
- Department of Homeland Security on First Responders: dhs.gov/science-and-technology/first-responders
- Everytown for Gun Safety: everytown.org
- Giffords: giffords.org
- Moms Demand Action: momsdemandaction.org
- National Education Association: nea.org
- Native Land App: native-land.ca
- Personal Budgeting: mint.com

Jessica Jollie is the daughter of two retired civil servants, an enrolled member of Comanche Nation, and a graduate of Yale College. She graduated with a degree in Art History, but has since devoted her time and talents to progressive, political campaigns. She has worked in organizing and operations for presidential candidates, state political parties, and environmental cause campaigns, calling many different cities and small towns around the U.S. home.